Colonization and Native Peoples

by J. Matteson Claus

Scott Foresman
is an imprint of

PEARSON

Glenview, Illinois • Boston, Massachusetts • Chandler, Arizona
Upper Saddle River, New Jersey

Every effort has been made to secure permission and provide appropriate credit for photographic material. The publisher deeply regrets any omission and pledges to correct errors called to its attention in subsequent editions.

Unless otherwise acknowledged, all photographs are the property of Scott Foresman, a division of Pearson Education.

Photo locators denoted as follows: Top (T), Center (C), Bottom (B), Left (L), Right (R), Background (Bkgd)

Opener: ©CORBIS; 1 ©MPI/Getty Images; 4 ©Archivo Iconografico, S.A./CORBIS; 6 ©Archivo Iconografico, S.A./CORBIS; 8 ©Stapleton Collection/CORBIS; 10(Bkgd) ©CORBIS; 10(B) ©Peter Harholdt/CORBIS; 12 ©MPI/Getty Images; 13 ©Kean Collection/ Getty Images; 15 ©Bettmann/CORBIS; 16(Bkgd) ©L. Clarke/CORBIS; 16(C) ©Michael & Patricia Fogden/CORBIS; 17 ©Charles & Josette Lenars/CORBIS; 18 ©Bettmann/CORBIS; 19 ©Swim Ink 2, LLC/CORBIS; 20 ©Dave G. Houser/CORBIS; 21 ©CORBIS SYGMA; 22 ©Werner Forman/CORBIS

ISBN 13: 978-0-328-52690-1
ISBN 10:   0-328-52690-8

Copyright © by Pearson Education, Inc., or its affiliates. All rights reserved.
Printed in the United States of America. This publication is protected by copyright, and permission should be obtained from the publisher prior to any prohibited reproduction, storage in a retrieval system, or transmission in any form or by any means, electronic, mechanical, photocopying, recording, or likewise. For information regarding permissions, write to Pearson Curriculum Rights & Permissions, One Lake Street, Upper Saddle River, New Jersey 07458.

Pearson® is a trademark, in the U.S. and/or in other countries, of Pearson plc or its affiliates.

Scott Foresman® is a trademark, in the U.S. and/or in other countries, of Pearson Education, Inc., or its affiliates.

2 3 4 5 6 7 8 9 10 V0N4 13 12 11 10

Introduction

The history of human exploration and colonization is both stunning and disturbing. The spread of European civilization brought innumerable benefits for many European people; the impact on the **indigenous,** or native, people, however, has been staggering.

The Age of Discovery in the fifteenth century marked the beginning of European colonization of the "New World"—the Americas. The pattern of destruction established by the earliest military **conquests** would be repeated for centuries. One of these first conquests was the Spanish victory over the Aztecs.

The Aztec Empire at its height

The Aztecs

Aztec is a term that can refer to both the people who lived in the city of Tenochtitlán and, more generally, the native people living in central Mexico. The Aztec tribes migrated to central Mexico from the north. In 1325 one tribe of Aztecs, called the Mexica, built the city of Tenochtitlán (present-day Mexico City) on an island in the center of a lake.

War was an important part of Aztec culture for several reasons. Being a soldier meant that one was part of a privileged upper class. The Aztecs gained more wealth with each conquest, and they also took prisoners-of-war to use in human sacrifices that were part of Aztec religious rituals.

Religion and the Aztecs

The Aztecs were a religious people who held complex rituals involving drama, dance, and elaborate costumes. Senior priests were made up of nobles, and the chief priest was the emperor. The Aztecs worshipped approximately 1,600 gods—one for every aspect of life. They believed that the gods demanded human sacrifices.

Feeding the Population

The Aztecs were excellent farmers, whose farming methods were, in fact, more advanced than those of the Spaniards who would conquer them. In order to feed their large population, the Aztecs cultivated all available land as well as reclaimed land from the lake for crops. They even terraced the hillsides by cutting steplike levels into them on which they could plant.

By 1428, the city of Tenochtitlán formed a triple alliance with the nearby states of Texcoco and Tlacopan. By the 1500s, the warlike Aztecs were able to control a kingdom of millions of people.

When Cortés and his men were brought to the city of Tenochtitlán, its beauty and riches stunned them. The city held towering pyramids and exotic palaces. The city was huge—about 200,000 people lived there—yet it was spotlessly clean.

The Arrival of the Spanish

The Aztec priests warned the emperor, Montezuma, that they had seen portents that something was coming. In 1519, that something arrived in the form of Hernando Cortés and 500 Spanish soldiers. When the Aztecs saw the Spaniards, they thought the foreigners were gods.

Conquering the Aztecs

The Spanish conquistadors—or conquerors—came to enrich themselves. They wanted gold and glory. They saw the Aztecs had much gold and wealth, and the Spanish set out to conquer them. The Aztec warriors, who greatly outnumbered the Spanish invaders, fought with darts, bows, spears, slings, and stone-edged swords. These weapons were easily repelled, however, by the conquistadors' metal armor. In addition to the armor, the Spanish had superior weapons: cannons, muskets, and crossbows. They also rode horses. The Aztecs had never seen horses before and were terrified by the beasts.

Still, the Spanish would never have been able to defeat the Aztecs, who vastly outnumbered them, if they had not found eager comrades among the local tribes. These natives hated the Aztecs who had conquered them, and they were eager to fight back. Their numbers swelled the Spanish force to more than 15,000. It took months of hard fighting, street to street, but eventually the Spanish defeated the Aztecs at Tenochtitlán. More than 100,000 Aztecs died defending their city.

An example of Aztec pictorial writing

The Aftermath

With the Aztecs defeated, the Spaniards took control of the empire. They destroyed the city of Tenochtitlán and built a new, Spanish-style city on its ruins. The new city was named Mexico City. The Spaniards dominated the conquered Aztecs.

From Warrior to Slave

During the fighting, much of the Aztec gold mysteriously disappeared. Cortés was unable to give his soldiers the gold he had promised them, but he did reward his comrades with Aztec warriors as slaves. Cortés punished the once proud warriors for defending their city by branding them and condemning them to lives of servitude.

The Land

Cortés also rewarded his soldiers by giving them land. The slaves were forced to work the land while the masters reaped the benefits. Furthermore, much of what the slaves produced was sent back to Spain—and so, with all the food being shipped abroad or consumed by their masters, many Aztecs died from starvation. Slaves also died from mistreatment.

Alongside the conquistadors, missionaries arrived with Cortés. With the Aztec defeat, Aztec temples and idols were destroyed and human sacrifice was banned. Hundreds of thousands of natives were baptized in an attempt to convert them to Christianity.

Friars and priests began educating Aztec nobles. The nobles learned about Christianity and also how to read in Latin. They began writing in Latin and abandoned their own pictorial written language.

Disease

In addition to Christianity, the Spaniards brought new diseases with them. The Aztecs had never been exposed to European sicknesses and, therefore, had no immunity to them. Smallpox alone wiped out nearly half of the Aztec population. Measles, mumps, and the plague also obliterated entire villages.

By 1580, just 60 years after the Spaniards' arrival, between 80 and 95 percent of the indigenous population was dead from war, disease, starvation, and maltreatment. The population of Mexico continued to decline for another century.

The Native Americans

Nearly a century after Cortés landed in Mexico, the English started the first permanent English colony in North America. In many ways, they followed a pattern of conquest similar to the Spanish.

Who Were the Native People of Virginia?

The native people who lived in what is now Virginia did not live under a single rule. In fact, there were several Native American tribes in the area. The Powhatan and the Susquehannock lived near the coast; the Monacan and Manahoac lived in the area around what is now Richmond; the Cherokee lived in the area of the Great Smoky Mountains.

Life among the Native Americans of Virginia

The indigenous people of Virginia lived in wooden houses—either in dome-shaped wigwams or in oblong longhouses with roofs made of bark. The houses were grouped together in villages containing as many as a thousand people.

Food for the Villages

Each village cultivated its own farmland. Women and children did the farming, planting corn, beans, pumpkins, melons, and tobacco.

The men hunted the native animals, which included turkeys, bison, and deer. The Indians used almost every part of the animals they killed. The skins were used to make clothing, and the bones were honed into tools. Deer horns were even used to make glue.

Religion and the Native Americans

Like the Aztecs, Native Americans worshipped many gods including gods of the sun and moon. Similarly, Native American religion was rooted in nature. Prayer was an important part of Native American festivals, and rituals included games, music, singing, dancing, and storytelling.

War and the Native Americans

The indigenous people of Virginia were experienced fighters who had clear rules about war. They treated war like hunting: they would lie in wait for their prey, then attack their opponents unexpectedly. This was different from the European idea of warfare—an out-in-the-open fighting style.

The Arrival of the English

The English founded Jamestown, Virginia, in 1607. They planned their colony as a business investment. Many of the settlers were businessmen accustomed to having servants do all the work and were unprepared for the hardships of colonial life. They did not know how to farm, nor, except for their leader, John Smith, did they know how to hunt and fish. Also, they didn't know how to use the native plants of the new land. By the summer of 1607, they were running out of food.

To further complicate matters, the colonists had trouble with the native peoples who sporadically attacked their settlements.

Occasionally, the English convinced the Native Americans to trade with them. The early trading was **advantageous** to both groups. The English received desperately needed food, and the indigenous people were able to obtain goods like knives and cooking utensils. When they asked the English to trade "thunder sticks" (guns), however, the English refused.

Wahunsunacock, the paramount chief, called Powhatan, of some thirty tribes, knew the English had come to take the land. He captured John Smith, but Powhatan's daughter, Pocahontas, intervened and saved Smith's life. Powhatan and Smith forged a friendship, and for a while, the Powhatan people and the colonists lived in peace, with the native people teaching the colonists how to plant corn and trap fish.

The peace didn't last, however. John Smith had to return to England for health reasons and Pocahontas and Powhatan both died. Then, in 1622, Powhatan warriors attacked and massacred over 400 colonists. Fighting ensued for the next several decades, with extensive casualties on both sides. Still, English colonists kept arriving. The indigenous people were pushed back, and eventually most fled the area or were killed.

The Aftermath

Disease

Just like the Aztecs, the indigenous people of North America had never been exposed to the diseases brought by Europeans, and, again like the Aztecs, the native people of Virginia succumbed by the thousands to smallpox and other illnesses.

Land

Individual ownership of land was a concept foreign to Native Americans. They saw how English colonists came and claimed the land on which the native people had lived and hunted for generations. Some of the tribes fought for their lands. Sometimes the colonists were able to buy land from the Native Americans, but sometimes the colonists tricked the chiefs into signing treaties giving up their land. The colonists did not try to force the Native Americans into slavery, however, as the Spanish did with the Aztec.

Religion

In some cases, the English tried to convert Native Americans to Christianity. Pocahontas was baptized and became a Christian. Mostly, however, English settlers wished to displace the native peoples and take their land.

War

To a large extent, Native Americans of North Virginia suffered the same fate as the Aztecs: they were overcome by superior firepower and disease. Unlike the Aztecs, however, the native peoples of Virginia were also outnumbered. No matter how many English settlers they fought off, more arrived. A century after the Europeans' arrival, the Native American population was greatly reduced.

From a German print "People of Australia and Oceania," circa 1900

The Australian Aborigines

Nearly two hundred years after the English founded Jamestown in Virginia, they colonized Australia. Like the Americas, Australia had a native population. Unfortunately, the Aborigines, the name used collectively to describe many distinct groups of the native people of Australia, fared little better under colonization than their counterparts in Mexico and Virginia.

The most common theory is that the Aborigines began inhabiting Australia between 40,000 and 50,000 years ago. When the English arrived, there were approximately 200 separate Aborigine groups with many different languages and cultures.

Aborigine groups inhabited many different parts of the Australian continent. As a result, their way of life varied from place to place. In general, they were hunter-gatherers, hunting native animals such as kangaroos and lizards. Some Aborigine were fishermen. They also gathered and ate roots, fruits, and other plants.

Totems were symbols of the powerful aspects of a thing or place. For example, an animal totem represented the strengths of that animal.

The Dreamtime

Similar to the religions of the native people of the Americas, the Aborigine religion was rooted in nature. According to Aborigine beliefs, the time before the world was created was known as the Dreamtime. The mythical beings who lived during the Dreamtime created the world—the land, the plants, the animals, and the people. Then these beings were absorbed into the landscape so that their energies lived in the land. For this reason, the Aborigines felt connected to their land.

Their daily activities were also connected with spiritual life. Rituals and ceremonies kept the Aborigine people in touch with the Dreamtime, providing wisdom and strength. Tribes sometimes spent weeks preparing dances, music, chants, body painting, bark paintings, and wood totems.

Australia the Penal Colony

In 1788, Captain Arthur Phillip arrived from England with a fleet of ships with 730 prisoners and 200 British soldiers to keep them in line. Thus began Australian colonization—with a penal colony. Over the next 80 years, approximately 160,000 convicts were transported to Australia.

In addition to the convicts, settlers flowed into Australia. By the 1850s, Australia's European population had nearly tripled, from around 400,000 people to 1.1 million.

Effects on the Aborigines

As in the Americas, the influx of colonists had **devastating** effects on the native population. European settlers took lands that were vital to the Aborigines and also took water sources for their own exclusive use. In many areas, they destroyed previously fertile lands by turning loose their herds of sheep and cattle to graze. The loss of land was a harsh blow to the Aborigine way of life.

Religion

The English made little effort to convert the Aborigines to Christianity. Like the English settlers in Virginia, Australian colonizers really just wanted the land. To the Aborigines, their land was part of their identity. Their culture was deeply affected when they were displaced.

Displacing the Aborigines

At first, the Aborigines welcomed early colonists. When colonists claimed their lands, however, they fought back by stealing sheep. For the native people, loss of land meant loss of hunting grounds and, thus, loss of food.

The colonists responded with violence. Like the Native Americans, the Aborigines were no match for the Europeans and their guns. The Aborigine people tried to fight back with spears, but many were **massacred**. As recently as 1928, Australian settlers were still killing Aborigine people.

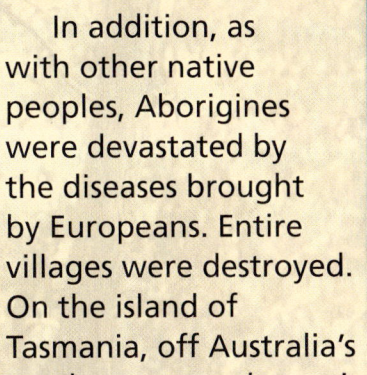

In addition, as with other native peoples, Aborigines were devastated by the diseases brought by Europeans. Entire villages were destroyed. On the island of Tasmania, off Australia's southern coast, the entire Aborigine population was obliterated in the 1800s from a combination of disease, displacement, and murder.

The Results

By the early twentieth century, the Australian Aborigine population had been reduced by 90 percent. As in Mexico and Virginia, the arrival of colonists in Australia proved to be deadly to the indigenous population.

Aztecs, Native Americans, and Aborigines Today

The indigenous populations never really recovered from colonization. However, each population continued on in its own way.

When Mexico declared independence from Spain in 1822, it embraced its Aztec past. Some of the Aztec religion survived as well—for example, the Mexican holiday known as The Day of the Dead comes from ancient Aztec practices.

In the United States, the Native American struggle didn't end in Virginia. Eventually, settlers in the United States displaced or conquered all the Native Americans. Those who survived were forced to live on reservations. Today, Native Americans battle difficulties from unemployment to alcoholism. Popular attitudes are changing, however, and Native American culture is now viewed with more respect. Modern tribes are creating more opportunities for themselves while retaining or re-establishing their identities.

In Australia, Aborigine people were also sent to reservations. However, in 1976 they were awarded one-fourth of the Northern Territories in Australia. It wasn't until 1993, though, that they won the right to make territorial claims in court. Like the Native Americans, the Australian Aborigines remain one of the most disadvantaged groups in their nation. In 1988, Australia celebrated its 200th anniversary, but the Aborigines declared it a year of mourning.

Native Americans dance at a powwow in Montana, 1994. (Inset) A Yanomami woman of Brazil, dressed for a ceremony

Conclusion

The history of human colonization is both inspiring and sobering. On the one hand, it is a huge achievement to have successfully colonized so many of the varied lands and environments of our planet. On the other hand, the wake of destruction left behind by this colonization is cause for serious thought.

Almost 270 years separated the colonization of Mexico and Australia, but in both cases, the effects were the same. Sadly, the same mistakes are made today. Modern indigenous populations such as the Yanomami in Brazil are being destroyed as outsiders attempt to claim their land.

Once destroyed, the culture and knowledge of native peoples are lost forever.

Now Try This

One of the challenges faced by explorers confronting native people was the language barrier. When settlers reached Mexico, Virginia, and Australia, they had to learn how to communicate with the indigenous tribes.

One way to communicate is through pictures. The Aztec scribes used picture writing that was bound in books called codices. These books were a bit like modern comic books—the pictures told the story. Unlike modern books, however, Aztec books were bound on both sides.

When pictures are used in writing, they are often used as symbols. For example, an eye might not only represent an eye but might also represent vision or seeing.

Here's How to Do It!

Create your own codex. See if you can effectively convey a story using pictures. You can either draw your own symbols and pictures or cut pictures from other sources. Make sure your story has a beginning, middle, and end.

1. Write a story outline.
   - Make an outline of actions or images that complete a story sequence.
   - Make sure your story has a beginning, middle, and end.

2. Decide on symbols that stand for people or events.
   - Draw pictures that tell your story
   - Or, cut out pictures from other sources.
   - Create some order to your pictures so that your readers can follow your story.

3. Include a legend to explain your codex symbols to your readers.
   - For example, ≈≈≈ = water, and so on.

Have fun and good luck!

Glossary

advantageous *adj.* giving a benefit; favorable

conquests *n.* acts of winning in war; taking by force

counterparts *n.* people or things that closely resemble other people or things

devastating *adj.* causing destruction

immunity *n.* resistance to disease, poison, etc.

indigenous *adj.* originating in a particular country

massacred *v.* killed needlessly or cruelly

penal *adj.* of, about, or given as punishment

portents *n.* warnings, usually of coming evil; omens